QUIZPEDIA

AMY LEWIS

D0168774

THE OFFICE

THE ULTIMATE BOOK OF TRIVIA

Smith Street Books

SO YOU THINK
YOU KNOW ...

SEASON

ONE

Quiz 01

1.

In the pilot episode, what nickname does Michael give to Jan?

2.

On Diversity Day, what "races" does Dwight claim he is attracted to?

3.

Jim and Pam make up a disease to fool Dwight, claiming that it makes one's teeth turn to liquid and drip down the back of one's throat. What do they call this disease?

4.

What color does Angela declare to be "whoreish"?

5.

While playing basketball, Michael is hit in the face. What kind of foul does he claim to have been a victim of?

6.

Who does Michael ask to be cheerleader for the basketball game?

7.

What does "Hot Girl" Katy sell from the conference room?

8.

Michael offers a $1000 prize for the best salesman, but ends up spending the money on what object to impress Katy?

9.

Where does Michael "file" messages from Dunder Mifflin corporate?

10.

In "The Alliance", what does Dwight hide in while trying to gather information in the warehouse?

SO YOU THINK
YOU KNOW ...

SEASON
TWO

"I'M AN EARLY BIRD,
AND I'M A NIGHT OWL.
SO I'M WISE AND I
HAVE WORMS"

Quiz 02

1.
What is the name of the game that Angela makes up, where she counts how many times Pam walks over to Jim's desk?

2.
When Creed convinces Michael to fire Devon, what does Devon throw at Michael's car in retaliation?

3.
Where do we learn that Roy left Pam behind on their first date?

4.
What is the name of the hero in *Threat Level Midnight*?

5.
What does Phyllis give Michael for Secret Santa?

6.
In Michael's improv class, what item does he constantly pretend to be holding?

7.
What is the name of the video that Michael presents to the new CFO of Dunder Mifflin?

8.
What is the name of the children's TV show that Michael appeared on as a small boy?

9.
What did Michael smoke at an Alicia Keys concert that makes him worry he will fail a drug test?

10.
Where does Toby store Dwight's HR complaints against Jim?

SO YOU THINK
YOU KNOW ...

SEASON
THREE

Quiz 03

1.
Where does Phyllis take Karen before they start their sales day trip?

2.
What computer game do the Stamford team play competitively?

3.
What is the name of the orientation video that Michael once made to encourage people to label their food in the office?

4.
Just back from vacation, what does Michael want the team to start having each day at 3 pm?

5.
What color do Dwight and Andy paint Michael's office, believing that he will get the job in New York?

6.
When Roy comes to confront Jim about kissing Pam, how does Dwight stop him?

7.
While at the mall, what does Michael offer to buy the women of the office to celebrate "Women's Appreciation"?

8.
What is the real first name of the Benjamin Franklin impersonator that comes to the office?

9.
What is the name of Michael's convict character?

10.
When Dwight temporarily leaves Dunder Mifflin, where does he get a job?

SO YOU THINK
YOU KNOW ...

SEASON

FOUR

Quiz 04

1.
What disease is the fun run in aid of?

2.
What pasta dish does Michael eat to carbo-load just before starting the fun run?

3.
When Pam and Jim stay at Schrute Farms, what popular book series does Dwight read to them as a bedtime story?

4.
What are the two similarly named, but vastly differing in quality pizza restaurants in Scranton?

5.
What author rejects Phyllis' invitation to participate in a local TV ad for Dunder Mifflin?

6.
The Finer Things Club was founded by Pam, Oscar and who?

7.
When Dwight plays *Second Life*, his character is exactly the same as his real-life self, in all aspects except one. What is it?

8.
What is the name of the security guard, which Jim forgets after he locks the team in the office?

9.
At the job fair, what single item does Michael place on the Dunder Mifflin display table?

10.
What is written on the rock that Michael gives to Toby as a farewell present?

SO YOU THINK YOU KNOW ...

SEASON FIVE

"HOLLY, YOU AND I ARE SOUP SNAKES"

Quiz 05

1.
What shape is Andy and Angela's planned wedding cake?

2.
When Michael discovered YouTube, how many days did he take off work?

3.
What are the "drugs" that Michael hides in Toby's drawer to try and frame him after his trip to Costa Rica?

4.
What party favors did Kelly give out at her *America's Got Talent* party, that Michael was not invited to?

5.
Where does David Wallace send Michael to on a business trip?

6.
In "Employee Transfer", what does Phyllis dress as for Halloween?

7.
How much does Kevin think that Pam weighs, after she jumps off the industrial scale?

8.
What Dunder Mifflin branch does Karen become the manager of?

9.
After Michael quits and gives his two weeks' notice, what is the first paper company he calls for a job?

10.
On Casual Friday, what does Oscar wear that Angela makes a complaint to Toby about?

SEASON SIX

Quiz 06

1.
What is Stanley's wife's name?

2.
What object does Dwight hide a listening device inside of, to eavesdrop on Jim's conversations?

3.
What does Michael fall into when out at a business meeting with Jim, that is captured on CCTV?

4.
What is the name of the bar manager that Michael has a fling with?

5.
When Sabre takes over Dunder Mifflin, which celebrity stars in the promotional video that is shown to the team?

6.
When Pam is in labor, what does Kevin suggest "sticking up her butt" to move things along faster?

7.
What beloved TV puppet features in the parody video that Oscar creates to make fun of Kevin?

8.
How many nights in the hospital does Jim and Pam's healthcare insurance cover?

9.
Which member of the warehouse does Oscar develop a crush on?

10.
What does Michael learn about Pam's mother that makes him stop dating her?

SO YOU THINK YOU KNOW ...

SEASON SEVEN

Quiz 07

1.
What disease does Michael catch on his summer break before Season 7 commences?

2.
What is the name of the day care center that Dwight sets up in the building?

3.
Who does Gabe dress up as for the costume contest?

4.
What is the name of Michael's autobiography?

5.
What is the key ingredient in the Chinese virility supplement that Gabe takes?

6.
What is the password for the Dunder Mifflin server?

7.
What is the name of Ryan's new internet startup?

8.
Which band's t-shirt is Cece baptized in, after getting her baptism outfit dirty?

9.
What is Kelly's New Year's resolution?

10.
Deangelo Vickers says that baby Cece could star in the show called what?

SEASON EIGHT

Quiz 08

1.
What holiday weekend does Andy ask Robert California to leave a half day early for?

2.
What is the name of Sabre's new tablet?

3.
What is Gabe's middle name?

4.
When Jim describes what he would do if he won the lottery, what does his fantasy sound like to Pam?

5.
What type of party does Andy throw to impress Robert?

6.
Which Starcraft character does Dwight come dressed as for Halloween?

7.
When Gabe asks Val out, what does he say his plans are for the evening?

8.
When the team heads off on a field trip to Gettysburg, what is written on the pink hats that Andy hands out?

9.
What is the name of Oscar's trivia team?

10.
When Pam returns from maternity leave, what does Andy mime doing to her now that she's "not pregnant"?

SO YOU THINK
YOU KNOW ...

SEASON
NINE

"I WORKED FOR A PAPER COMPANY ALL THESE YEARS AND I NEVER WROTE ANYTHING DOWN"

Quiz 09

1.
What does Pam create to keep things in order when the building's custodian goes on holiday?

2.
When Jim convinces Dwight that the office is unsafe, what alternative work space does Dwight provide?

3.
Who is Senator Lipton cheating on Angela with?

4.
When the team contracts lice, what do they put in their hair to get rid of the infestation?

5.
What family event does Jim miss while he is stuck working in Philadelphia?

6.
Which member of the warehouse team draws on Pam's mural?

7.
Which relative of Dwight's dies, whom he says was the closest person he had to a mother?

8.
What audiobook does Phyllis listen to during the working day?

9.
When Dwight's karate master comes to the office, what ceremony does he perform?

10.
What song does Andy perform on *America's Next A Cappella Sensation*?

SO YOU THINK
YOU KNOW ...

THE
DUNDIES

Quiz 10

1.
In Season 2, what song does Michael rap over at the beginning of The Dundies?

2.
For how many years running did Ryan win the Hottest in The Office Award?

3.
In Season 2, which Dundie does Michael award Phyllis?

4.
Which Dundie did Pam win for many years at Dunder Mifflin, only to have it replaced with the Whitest Sneakers Award?

5.
In Season 2, which embarrassing Dundie does Kevin get awarded?

6.
When Kelly is given the Spicy Curry Award what is on top of the trophy?

7.
In Season 7, which Dundie does Michael give to Andy after learning that he tried marijuana in college?

8.
Which Dundie do we learn that Michael once gave Toby?

9.
What does Stanley do with his Dundie trophies each year?

10.
What awkward question does Deangelo Vickers ask when Michael is training him on how to be a good Dundies host and interact with the audience?

SO YOU THINK
YOU KNOW ...

THE
OFFICE
LOCATIONS

Quiz 11

1.

After a business meeting, outside what restaurant does Michael charm Jan in to going home with him?

2.

Where was the original location for the meeting mentioned above?

3.

Where does Michael take the team for Beach Day?

4.

What Japanese restaurant do Michael, Jim, Andy and Dwight visit, only to return to the office Christmas party with two of the waitresses?

5.

What does Michael claim Times Square is named for?

6.

What is the name of the bar that Roy and his brother trash after he finds out Pam and Jim kissed?

7.

What is the name of the fun run that Michael organizes in honor of Meredith?

8.

Where does Michael run into his real estate agent Carol and her kids?

9.

What restaurant does Michael take Jim to, to discuss Jim's feelings for Pam?

10.

What restaurant in New York does Michael claim makes the best pizza?

THE

OFFICE

INCIDENTS

AND

ACCIDENTS

Quiz 12

1.
When a bat is found in the office, Dwight traps it in a garbage bag, along with who?

2.
When Michael hits Meredith with his car, what does Dwight claim the electricity used to keep her alive could power for two days instead?

3.
What is the cause of Stanley's heart attack?

4.
What does Angela throw to Oscar, who has climbed into the ceiling, when she believes the office is on fire?

5.
Who kicked a ladder out from under Darryl?

6.
When Jim signs Meredith's pelvis cast, what name does he sign?

7.
How does Dwight get a concussion, while trying to rush to Michael's aid after he burns his foot?

8.
When Andy video calls the office from his boat after two days at sea, he appears to be going mad and suffering from what injury?

9.
What two animals has Meredith been bitten by, other than a bat?

10.
How does Michael plan to prove that work-induced depression is dangerous?

SO YOU THINK YOU KNOW ...

THE HISTORY OF DUNDER MIFFLIN

Quiz 13

1.
When Robert Dunder comes to Michael's ageism presentation, how does he reveal that Mifflin died?

2.
In what year was Dunder Mifflin founded?

3.
What did the company sell before it sold paper?

4.
Why was the Dunder Mifflin Pittsfield branch shut down?

5.
Since what year has the original Dunder Mifflin website been "under construction"?

6.
Who replaces Pam as receptionist when she goes to study in New York City?

7.
What company is the Dunder Mifflin warehouse originally on lease from?

8.
How did Michael's former boss Ed Truck die?

9.
How many regional managers does Dunder Mifflin have over the course of *The Office*?

10.
What is the Dunder Mifflin three-letter stock symbol?

THE MANY MANAGERS OF DUNDER MIFFLIN

Quiz 14

1.
What song plays while Deangelo Vickers does his juggling mime for the office?

2.
What is Deangelo doing when he injures himself, resulting in hospitalization?

3.
What are Robert California's two favorite songs, according to a mean email sent by Jim?

4.
What type of "young women" does Robert plan to mentor in Europe when he leaves Dunder Mifflin?

5.
What is the title of Jo Bennett's autobiography?

6.
What famous author has Jo "slept with the same three guys" as?

7.
What industry did Charles Miner work in before joining Dunder Mifflin?

8.
What is Charles' favorite sport?

9.
What town in England did Nellie Bertram grow up in?

10.
What job does Nellie give Andy out of sympathy, after he gets fired from Dunder Mifflin?

SO YOU THINK
YOU KNOW ...

THE
OFFICE
CELEBRITY
GUESTS

Quiz 15

1.
Which actress plays Katy, who we first meet in the episode "Hot Girl"?

2.
Jim Carrey plays an interviewee for the manager of Dunder Mifflin. What area in the USA does he repeatedly mention?

3.
In "The Seminar", which writer of the original *The Office* series guest stars?

4.
Who guest stars as Merv Bronte, the candidate who eats during his interview to be the new manager?

5.
Who guest stars as Andy's brother Walter Bernard Jr?

6.
Which cast member from *Glee* guest stars as a pizza delivery guy?

7.
Which *Saturday Night Live* cast members are shown taunting Andy's viral a cappella video?

8.
What comedian appears as Michael's improv classmate?

9.
Stephen Colbert guest stars as which member of Andy's band Here Comes Treble?

10.
What two actors guest star as Erin's mother and father in the finale of the series?

THE OFFICE ROMANCES

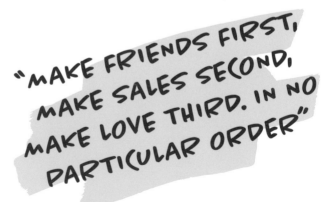

"MAKE FRIENDS FIRST, MAKE SALES SECOND, MAKE LOVE THIRD. IN NO PARTICULAR ORDER"

Quiz 16

1.
What is Dwight's romantic pet name for Angela?

2.
What does Dwight give to Angela's cat Sprinkles to euthanize it?

3.
Who does Erin begin to have feelings for while Andy is away on his boat trip?

4.
At Angela and Andy's mock wedding, what is the ring that Dwight gives her made of?

5.
What color does Jan insist Michael change his bedroom walls to, instead of white?

6.
When Ryan breaks up with Kelly and suggests they have sex one more time, what else does he ask her for?

7.
How does Kelly break up with Darryl, with Ryan's assistance?

8.
What is the name of Jan's assistant Hunter's band?

9.
What tattoo does Gabe get, that he claims he got for Erin?

10.
What is the name of the cat that Oscar adopts from Angela, to help relieve his guilt for sleeping with Angela's partner?

SO YOU THINK YOU KNOW ...

THE OFFICE CHRISTMAS PARTIES

Quiz 17

1.
In Season 2, what expensive item does Michael place in the Secret Santa game?

2.
In "A Benihana Christmas", what is the theme of the party that Pam and Karen organize?

3.
What song do Andy and Michael serenade the Benihana waitresses with?

4.
What toy does Dwight buy in bulk to sell to desperate parents?

5.
Michael pretends he is driving Meredith to a bar after one of the office Christmas parties. Where is he really trying to take her?

6.
What do the French hens that Andy gives to Erin on the 12 days of Christmas do to her?

7.
When Phyllis dresses up as the office Santa, who does Michael come dressed as because he is jealous?

8.
Where does Dwight hide when he ambushes Jim with snowballs in the parking lot?

9.
In "Christmas Wishes", what does Dwight put in his own office drawer and tries to pin the blame on Jim?

10.
In "Dwight Christmas", what is the theme that Dwight chooses?

MICHAEL
AND
JAN

Quiz 18

1.
What holiday resort does Michael take Jan to?

2.
What is the name of the file that Michael saves the photo of Jan topless on the beach as?

3.
Which branch manager reveals that Michael and Jan slept together?

4.
How many wine glasses do Michael and Jan own?

5.
What magazine does Michael claim the photo of himself and Jan in Jamaica could be shown in?

6.
What does Michael refer to Jan's new breast implants as?

7.
What is Michael and Jan's safe word when they are making love?

8.
In Season 4, Michael trades in his car to buy what for Jan?

9.
In the episode "Women's Appreciation", what two things does Michael tell the team that Jan does that makes him uncomfortable?

10.
Who takes Michael home after he quarrels with Jan at their dinner party?

SO YOU THINK YOU KNOW ...

PAM AND JIM

"YOU ARE EVERYTHING"

Quiz 19

1.
When Jim buys his parents' house to surprise Pam, what is permanently stuck to one of the walls in the hallway?

2.
What item does Jim place a selection of in-joke gifts inside for Pam's Secret Santa?

3.
At what work event do Jim and Pam have their first kiss?

4.
At what location halfway between New York City and Scranton does Jim propose to Pam?

5.
Where do Pam and Jim get married?

6.
What is the title of the memo that Toby sends out because he is jealous of Pam and Jim?

7.
Where do Pam and Jim go on their honeymoon?

8.
What is the name of the documentary cameraman that takes a liking to Pam in later seasons?

9.
How long did Jim wait once they started dating to buy Pam an engagement ring?

10.
What are the names of Pam and Jim's two children?

KELLY

AND

RYAN

Quiz 20

1.
What day of the year do Kelly and Ryan first hook up?

2.
What does Ryan realize that the definition of "having fun" for Kelly is?

3.
Why does Ryan break up with Kelly the first time?

4.
Who does Ryan claim that he rejected because he was committed to Kelly?

5.
Who does Kelly imply that Ryan is flirting with to cause problems in the office?

6.
Who does Kelly date after Ryan, to make him jealous?

7.
What does Ryan do on the office floor to try to impress Kelly?

8.
Where does Ryan plan to go on his trip after dumping Kelly and having sex "one more time"?

9.
What does Ryan point at when he says to Kelly "that will be the color of our children"?

10.
What state does Ryan follow Kelly to when she gets engaged to Ravi?

SO YOU THINK
YOU KNOW ...

MICHAEL
AND
HOLLY

Quiz 21

1.
Who does Holly replace when she joins the team at Dunder Mifflin?

2.
How many days after meeting Holly does Michael decide that he loves her?

3.
What concert does Holly buy tickets for to take her yoga instructor to, but ends up selling to Michael who then tears them up?

4.
When Michael goes to Nashua to surprise Holly, where is she?

5.
What is the name of Holly's boyfriend in Nashua?

6.
Michael destroys Holly's boyfriend's Christmas gift. What is it?

7.
What is the name of the skit that Michael and Holly put on at the company picnic?

8.
What item does Holly convince Michael to keep during the office garage sale?

9.
Where do Michael and Holly first make love?

10.
What does Michael claim is the guideline for how much you should spend on an engagement ring?

SO YOU THINK
YOU KNOW ...

DWIGHT SCHRUTE

Quiz 22

1.
Why was Dwight shunned by his family between the ages of four and six?

2.
What is the name of Dwight's cousin who lives with him on the beet farm?

3.
The three different themed rooms at the Schrute Farms bed and breakfast are America, Irrigation and what?

4.
During traditional Schrute weddings, what do the bride and groom stand in?

5.
What is Dwight's great grandfather's name?

6.
What type of karate does Dwight have a black belt in?

7.
What type of car does Dwight drive?

8.
According to Dwight, what age is his Grandpa Manheim?

9.
How many cousins does Dwight have?

10.
What surgery does Dwight claim to have performed on himself as a child?

SO YOU THINK
YOU KNOW ...

ANGELA
MARTIN

Quiz 23

1.
When Dwight kills Angela's cat Sprinkles, where does he place the body?

2.
What department is Angela the head of?

3.
What is the name of the state senator that Angela marries?

4.
What is Angela's clothing size?

5.
What name does Angela book a hotel room under when following Dwight to the office supply convention?

6.
What is the book that Angela claims she would take to a desert island simply for the purpose of burning it?

7.
What does Angela define as "first base" with a man?

8.
What is the agreed settlement for Angela and Dwight's baby contract?

9.
What does Angela claim she weighs, when asking Oscar to rescue her in the "Stress Relief" episode?

10.
Why does Angela spit out a cookie at the Moroccan Christmas party?

CREED
BRATTON

"JUST PRETEND LIKE WE'RE TALKING UNTIL THE COPS LEAVE"

Quiz 24

1.
What kind of car does Creed drive?

2.
What is the name of Creed's blog that Ryan sets up for him in Microsoft Word?

3.
What medical condition does Creed fear will prevent him from achieving his dream of scuba diving?

4.
What is Creed's favorite birthday dessert?

5.
Creed refers to the Taliban as "the worst". What positive thing does he have to say about them?

6.
What does Creed use to dye his hair, after being told by Ryan that the company is getting younger and more dynamic?

7.
What name is on Creed's passport?

8.
What does Creed grow in his desk drawer, which emits an "old man smell"?

9.
What are the two things that a person can "ooze", according to Creed?

10.
How many toes does Creed have on his right foot?

SO YOU THINK
YOU KNOW ...

TOBY
FLENDERSON

Quiz 25

1.
What is Toby's daughter's name?

2.
What type of novel is Toby writing?

3.
Where did Toby claim to have met the woman he brought as a date to Phyllis' wedding?

4.
Much to his embarrassment, what does Toby accidentally touch when the team is locked in the office, waiting for a security guard to let them out?

5.
What time and day of the week did Michael hold Toby's birthday party, according to Toby?

6.
Where does Toby decide to move to in Season 4?

7.
What happens to Toby on his trip, resulting in him being hospitalized for a broken neck?

8.
What local case is Toby assigned to the jury of?

9.
Which Dunder Mifflin regional manager does Toby have a crush on, despite the feelings not being reciprocated?

10.
What happens to Toby when he visits the Scranton Strangler in prison?

SO YOU THINK
YOU KNOW ...

ANDY BERNARD

Quiz 26

1.
What is the name of Andy's singing group?

2.
What does Jim do to Andy that exposes Andy's issues with anger management for the first time in the Stamford office?

3.
What is the nickname that Andy gives himself, which he later gets a tattoo of to match?

4.
Who replaces Andy as Regional Manager of Scranton when he is in Florida?

5.
At which office member's farewell party does Andy propose to Angela?

6.
What Ivy League University did Andy attend?

7.
What is the name of the reality TV show that Andy auditions for, the footage of which goes viral?

8.
What does Andy lose during the pool party at Robert California's house?

9.
What local Scranton play does Andy get a role in?

10.
What does Deangelo Vickers ask Andy to drink in order to entertain him?

SO YOU THINK
YOU KNOW ...

KEVIN
MALONE

Quiz 27

1.
What dish does Kevin cook for his colleagues, and then accidentally spills all over the office carpet?

2.
How many women did Kevin propose to before his engagement to Stacy?

3.
What band was Kevin in before he joined Scrantonicity?

4.
For the costume contest, what famous American does Kevin come dressed as?

5.
What does Kevin win a gold medal for in the Office Olympics?

6.
In what season does Kevin announce that he has split from Stacy?

7.
Which team member is falsely led to believe Kevin is only at the office due to a "special work program"?

8.
What is the name of the woman that Kevin meets during the blood drive, but is nervous about talking to?

9.
In the series finale, we learn that Kevin has bought a what?

10.
What is Kevin's favorite number, which he also sets the office thermostat to?

JAN LEVINSON

Quiz 28

1.
According to Dwight, what store in Scranton does Jan like to buy clothes from?

2.
What is the title of the song that Jan's assistant Hunter records and gives her on CD?

3.
Jan releases an album covering the songs of which famous singer?

4.
What is the name of Jan's candle business?

5.
What are the two things David Wallace complains that Jan did in her office all day?

6.
What is the name of the baby that Jan has, without telling Michael?

7.
What is the name of the piano singing character that Jan plays in Michael's movie?

8.
Where does Jan say she was while she was with Michael in Jamaica?

9.
Where does Jan end up working at the end of the series?

10.
What does Jan claim that Michael is "above average" at?

SO YOU THINK
YOU KNOW ...

THE BOOZE
CRUISE

Quiz 29

1.
When Jim puts Dwight's personal items in the office vending machine, how much does the stapler cost?

2.
What lake does the booze cruise happen on?

3.
When Michael asks for a boat analogy for the sales department, what does Darryl suggest?

4.
In the same analogy, what does he suggest should be saved first?

5.
What excuse to leave does Pam use when her conversation with Jim on the deck is about to get serious?

6.
What is the name of the captain of the booze cruise?

7.
How long does Pam reveal she has been engaged to Roy for, while she is chatting to Jim's date?

8.
When Roy loudly announces setting a date for their wedding, what date does he suggest?

9.
When Michael is seasick, what does Dwight tell him that the captain recommends to help reduce the symptoms?

10.
What does the captain resort to doing to stop Michael from disrupting the cruise?

THE

INJURY

Quiz 30

1.
How does Michael injure his foot, before calling Pam in the office for help?

2.
What does Michael ask Ryan to bring to his house?

3.
Who does Dwight start being nice to in the office, which makes the team believe he might have a concussion?

4.
What does Michael ask Pam to rub on his foot?

5.
Where does Jim tell Dwight he is taking him in Meredith's minivan, when he is actually driving him to the hospital?

6.
Who parked in the wheelchair users space and made Billy Merchant late to Michael's talk?

7.
Where does Ryan end up driving to in order to find Michael's favorite pudding cups?

8.
What does Ryan sneak into Michael's pudding cup to stop him from complaining?

9.
Who does Dwight mistake Creed for while concussed?

10.
What does Michael do at the hospital that gets him told off by the lab technician?

CASINO

NIGHT

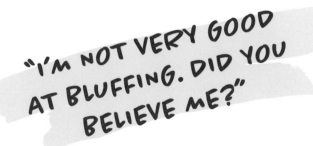

"I'M NOT VERY GOOD
AT BLUFFING. DID YOU
BELIEVE ME?"

Quiz 31

1.
What is the prize that Creed wins for having the highest chip count?

2.
Who does Pam call after Jim confesses his love for her?

3.
What tell does Jim enact during poker to make Dwight think he has a good hand?

4.
Who owned the suit that Dwight wears to Casino Night?

5.
What special skill does Jim convince Dwight he has, with the help of Pam?

6.
What charity does Michael choose to support with the money raised on the night?

7.
Who caters the food for Casino Night?

8.
Michael claims that JFK, the Holocaust and AIDS are unable to be joked about. Whose assassination does he say has "recently become funny"?

9.
What drink does Kelly ask Ryan to get for her?

10.
What is the name of Kevin's band?

PHYLLIS' WEDDING

Quiz 32

1.
Jim trains Dwight to salivate whenever he restarts his computer. What food does he use?

2.
Stanley brings the same wedding gift as Jim and Karen. What is it?

3.
When Dwight meets Angela before the ceremony, who does he say she looks as beautiful as?

4.
Why was Michael replaced by a dog as ring bearer at his mother's wedding to her partner, Jeff?

5.
Who goes missing at the wedding reception?

6.
Phyllis uses the same wedding invitation design as Pam and Roy's planned wedding. What other two things does she copy?

7.
Complete this sentence from Michael's speech "Webster's dictionary defines wedding as ..."

8.
What does Michael claim Phyllis' nickname was in high school?

9.
What song does Pam watch Jim and Karen slow dance to?

10.
What does Michael do to redeem himself after being thrown out of the wedding by Bob Vance?

SO YOU THINK
YOU KNOW ...

BUSINESS
SCHOOL

Quiz 33

1.
What is the "most inspiring thing" that Michael has ever said to Dwight?

2.
What does Dwight find trapped in the vent after finding "animal stool" in the office?

3.
What does Michael do at the start of his speech at Ryan's business school that horrifies the students?

4.
What are the "four kinds of businesses", according to Michael?

5.
Why can't Toby attend Pam's art show?

6.
What cold item does Jim claim to have been burned by, in order to convince Dwight that he has been turned into a vampire?

7.
Michael buys one of Pam's paintings. What is it of?

8.
Instead of firing Ryan, what does Michael do to punish him for suggesting that Dunder Mifflin might someday go out of business?

9.
What kind of art does Oscar's boyfriend describe Pam's artwork as?

10.
When Pam hugs Michael after the disappointing art show, what does he have in his pocket?

DUNDER MIFFLIN INFINITY

Quiz 34

1.
Where does Dwight source the cat that he offers Angela, to replace Sprinkles?

2.
When Ryan asks if the team has any questions about the new website, what is Kelly's question?

3.
What item does Ryan give to each member of the sales team as part of the website launch?

4.
What does Kelly tell Ryan to convince him to go to dinner with her after work?

5.
What is Michael's version of "instant messaging" with clients?

6.
Where does the GPS in Michael's car lead him and Dwight to?

7.
Which celebrity does Ryan claim to have run in to while getting a sandwich in New York?

8.
Complete this quote from Dwight to Angela: "I just want to be friends ..."

9.
When Michael and Dwight go back to the client to take back their gift basket, which item has been eaten?

10.
Complete this Michael Scott quote, when he is telling off Ryan about using new technology: "Game, set ..."

SO YOU THINK
YOU KNOW ...

SURVIVOR MAN

Quiz 35

1.
Who does Ryan invite on his corporate wilderness retreat, much to Michael's dismay?

2.
Complete this Dwight quote: "It is better to be hurt by someone you know accidentally, than ..."

3.
What is the first thing Michael does with his knife when left alone in the wilderness?

4.
In addition to a knife, what item does Michael take with him on his *Survivor Man* challenge?

5.
Which members of the office's birthdays fall in Jim's unpopular idea of "Birthday Month"?

6.
What kind of cake does Creed claim he hates when discussing the birthday month celebration with Jim?

7.
How long does Michael complain he has been without food for, before singing "Happy Birthday" to himself in the woods?

8.
What does Michael refer to his self-constructed shelter as?

9.
When Dwight "rescues" Michael, what movie title is on the sweatshirt he gives to Michael to wear?

10.
What does Michael eat in the forest that forces Dwight to rescue him?

THE

DEPOSITION

Quiz 36

1.
When Michael is deposed as part of Jan's wrongful termination lawsuit, why does Michael suggest she was fired?

2.
What is written on the hot dog doodle that Pam gives Michael as a fake phone message in front of Ryan?

3.
What phrase does Michael use to memorize the word "pattern" as part of his deposition statement?

4.
While the deposition is in progress, which two people in the office have a ping pong tournament?

5.
How much money does Jan want to sue Dunder Mifflin for?

6.
Complete this Kelly quote from the ping pong competition: "Your mom is so fat ..."

7.
How does Michael describe the "timing" of Jan's breast augmentation?

8.
Who has Michael written is "just as hot as Jan but in a different way"?

9.
What item does Jan bring as evidence to the deposition, causing Michael great embarrassment?

10.
What kind words does David Wallace say about Michael that make him feel better?

SO YOU THINK
YOU KNOW ...

THE
DINNER
PARTY

"KINDA SORTA AN
OAKY AFTERBIRTH"

Quiz 37

1.
During the dinner party, Michael reveals that he does not share a bed with Jan. Where does he sleep?

2.
What excuse does Michael use for dipping his steak into his wine before chewing it?

3.
Dwight brings an uninvited date to dinner. How does he know her?

4.
How much did Michael's wall-mounted plasma screen TV cost him?

5.
What two dishes does Dwight bring to the party for only himself and his date to eat?

6.
What does Jan serve for dinner?

7.
What nickname do Michael and Jan use for each other during the dinner party?

8.
What excuse does Jim use for leaving early, only to be thwarted by Pam?

9.
The glass door in the condo is broken because Michael ran through it. What was his reason for running?

10.
Shown in a later-released deleted scene from the episode, which five people would be in Dwight's top five dinner party guests?

THE

LECTURE

CIRCUIT

Quiz 38

1.
Why does Pam agree to join Michael on the lecture circuit?

2.
What does Michael ask Karen when he sees that she is pregnant?

3.
Encouraged by Pam, where does Michael drive to instead of Rochester?

4.
Who temporarily replaces Angela and Phyllis as the Party Planning Committee?

5.
Why is Kelly mad at Jim and Dwight?

6.
How did Michael learn the Pledge of Allegiance?

7.
What are Karen and her husband dressed up as in a photo in her office?

8.
What are the office staff horrified to witness on Angela's home security camera?

9.
When presenting to the Nashua team, what are Michael's opening words?

10.
What activities do Jim and Dwight give Kelly a choice between to celebrate her birthday?

SO YOU THINK YOU KNOW ...

THE MICHAEL SCOTT PAPER COMPANY

Quiz 39

1.
Where is the first office of The Michael Scott Paper Company, before it was deemed to be illegal?

2.
What song is Michael playing in his car when he arrives for his first day at his new company?

3.
What can be heard through the walls of the office that Michael, Pam and Ryan share?

4.
What function does Michael organize to launch his new company?

5.
What business does Dwight tell Erin used to be on the Dunder Mifflin office site?

6.
What places do the four clocks on the wall of The Michael Scott Paper Company display the time for?

7.
What item are Pam and Ryan supposed to share at the new paper company?

8.
What shape are the pancakes that Michael gives away?

9.
What report does Charles ask Jim to put together about his clients that confuses Jim?

10.
What song do Dwight and Andy play in the break room, trying to impress Erin?

SO YOU THINK
YOU KNOW ...

SCOTT'S TOTS

Quiz 40

1.
What grade were the class in when Michael first promised them college tuition?

2.
What is the name of the charity that Michael started?

3.
What is the name of the room at the school that the students dedicated to him?

4.
Who awkwardly wins the anonymously voted Employee of the Month contest?

5.
What age does Michael say that he thought he'd first be a millionaire by?

6.
What does Michael offer the students in lieu of the money for college tuition?

7.
When Jim is accused of cheating in the Employee of the Month contest, what does Creed accuse Pam of lying about?

8.
What is written on the Employee of the Month cake?

9.
What does Michael offer the student who follows him out of the building after his presentation?

10.
What positive statistic does Erin tell Michael as they are driving home from the school?

SO YOU THINK
YOU KNOW ...

THREAT
LEVEL
MIDNIGHT

Quiz 41

1.
What character does Jim play in *Threat Level Midnight*?

2.
Who does the voiceover for the film, and what movie's style of narration does it imitate?

3.
What is the name of Michael Scarn's dead wife?

4.
Who plays the president in *Threat Level Midnight*?

5.
Creed plays Michael Scarn's hockey coach. What is his name?

6.
What is the name of the jazz club that Michael Scarn visits?

7.
What does Michael Scarn's nemesis threaten to do to his dead wife?

8.
Where is the bomb hidden?

9.
What was far and away the most expensive scene in the movie, that Michael Scott insists was essential?

10.
What does Scarn say to his nemesis before he gets shot?

THE GARAGE SALE

Quiz 42

1.
What does Dwight trade Meredith for his thumb tack?

2.
What is the name of the "magic beans" that Jim tricks Dwight into buying?

3.
What does Michael initially plan on using to write his proposal to Holly?

4.
Whose image does Ryan put on the labels of his mother's pesto?

5.
What board game do Andy, Kevin and Darryl play for money?

6.
What does Phyllis tell Holly she has a box of stored under her table?

7.
What does Dwight swap Ryan's pesto for?

8.
What interrupts Michael's proposal to Holly in the annex?

9.
Whose voice does Michael impersonate when asking Holly to marry him?

10.
Where does Michael announce that he is moving to at the end of the episode?

SO YOU THINK
YOU KNOW ...

GOODBYE
MICHAEL

"THERE'S NOT ENOUGH
TIME IN THE DAY TO HAVE
A SPECIAL MOMENT WITH
EVERYBODY"

Quiz 43

1.
Who is the regional manager that takes over from Michael?

2.
What parting gift does Michael give to Phyllis?

3.
What is the topic of conversation in the lunchroom that pushes Michael to tears?

4.
Who does Michael give his neon bar sign to?

5.
What catchphrase does Michael say each time he tries to shoot a basket during his goodbye wander around the warehouse?

6.
What is Michael's one last wish to Darryl?

7.
What do Michael and Dwight do in the parking lot to celebrate his second-last day?

8.
What movie does Pam sneak off to when she should be out pricing a new shredder?

9.
Where does Gabe leave his love letter to Erin?

10.
What does Michael ask the cameraman to let him know, just before getting on the plane?

THE POOL PARTY

Quiz 44

1.
What does Jim hide in Dwight's desk to make Stanley laugh while Pam isn't around?

2.
Who suggests that Robert California should host a pool party at his house?

3.
What is Robert's ex-wife's name?

4.
What does Gabe say to interject himself into the conversation while Ryan is trying to bond with Robert?

5.
What is Robert's bed cover made of?

6.
What does Val ask Kevin which leads him to accuse her of being racist?

7.
What did Robert picture himself eating every night in his kitchen before he married a vegan?

8.
What three erotic movies did Robert buy for his home cinema?

9.
How did Erin know it was Andy's ring when she found it in the pool?

10.
What finally happens that makes Jim leave the party?

SO YOU THINK
YOU KNOW ...

THE
FINALE

Quiz 45

1.
What city has Darryl moved to, a year after the documentary airs?

2.
At Dwight's bachelor party, what does Dwight try to order from the stripper?

3.
Who carries Angela down the aisle at her wedding?

4.
At Angela's bachelorette party, who is the stripper?

5.
Where does Mose hide Angela during the bachelor party?

6.
What is the name of Ryan's baby?

7.
Who is the surprise guest that Jim invites to replace him as best man at the wedding?

8.
Complete this Michael Scott quote: "I feel like all my kids grew up ..."

9.
Where has Creed been living?

10.
What is the name of the mural that Pam paints and dedicates to Jim?

Answers

Quiz 01: 1. Hillary Rodham Clinton 2. White and Indian 3. Spontaneous Dental Hydroplosion 4. Green 5. A "flagrant, personal, intentional foul" 6. Pam 7. Purses 8. A coffee machine 9. The wastepaper basket 10. A cardboard box

Quiz 02: 1. Pam Pong 2. A pumpkin 3. A hockey game 4. Michael Scarn 5. A handmade oven mitt 6. A gun 7. "The Faces of Scranton" 8. *Fundle Bundle* 9. A clove cigarette 10. In a box under his desk.

Quiz 03: 1. A beauty salon 2. *Call of Duty* 3. "The Scranton Witch Project" 4. Pina coladas 5. Black 6. He pepper sprays him 7. One item from Victoria's Secret 8. Gordon 9. Prison Mike 10. Staples

Quiz 04: 1. Rabies 2. Fettuccine Alfredo 3. Harry Potter 4. Alfredo's Pizza Cafe and Pizza by Alfredo 5. Sue Grafton 6. Toby 7. He can fly 8. Hank 9. A single sheet of blank paper 10. "Suck on this"

Quiz 05: 1. A sailboat 2. Five 3. A Caprese salad 4. A mug with your own face on it 5. Winnipeg, Manitoba 6. Raggedy Ann 7. 226 pounds 8. Utica 9. Prince Paper 10. Sandals

Quiz 06: 1. Teri 2. A wooden mallard 3. A koi pond 4. Donna 5. Christian Slater 6. Spicy food 7. Cookie Monster 8. Two 9. Matt 10. She's 58.

Quiz 07: 1. West Nile virus 2. Sesame Avenue Day Care Center for Infants and Toddlers 3. Lady Gaga 4. *Somehow I Manage* 5. Powdered seahorse 6. bigboobz 7. WUPHF. com 8. Arcade Fire 9. To get more attention by any means necessary 10. *Babies I Don't Care About*

Quiz 08: 1. Columbus Day 2. Pyramid 3. Susan 4. Like they are Stephen King characters 5. A garden party 6. Kerrigan 7. To go to a cemetery and drink wine 8. DM does GB 9. Aesop's Foibles 10. Punching her in the stomach

Quiz 09: 1. The chore wheel 2. A bus 3. Oscar 4. Mayonnaise 5. Cece's ballet recital 6. Frank 7. Aunt Shirley 8. *Fifty Shades of Grey* 9. The changing of the belts 10. The Cornell fight song

Quiz 10: 1. "O.P.P." by Naughty by Nature 2. Six years (2005–2010) 3. Busiest Beaver Award (misspelled as Bushiest Beaver) 4. Longest Engagement Award 5. "Don't Go in There After Me" Award 6. A tenpin bowler 7. The Doobie Doobie Pothead Stoner of the Year Award 8. Extreme Repulsiveness Award 9. He throws them in the trash. 10. "Where were you on September 11th?"

Quiz 11: 1. Chili's 2. The Radisson 3. Lake Scranton 4. Benihana 5. The good times you have when you're in it 6. Poor Richard's 7. Michael Scott's Dunder Mifflin Scranton Meredith Palmer Memorial Celebrity Rabies Awareness Pro-Am Fun Run Race for the Cure 8. The ice rink 9. Hooters 10. Sbarro

Quiz 12: 1. Meredith 2. A small fan 3. A fire drill 4. Her cat, Bandit 5. Michael 6. John Krasinski 7. By crashing his car into a pole 8. Sunburn 9. A raccoon and a rat 10. By jumping off the building

Quiz 13: 1. He shot himself in the head 2. 1949 3. Metal brackets 4. The staff tried to unionize 5. 2002 6. Ronni

7. Beekman Properties 8. He was decapitated in a car accident 9. Ten 10. DMI

Quiz 14: 1. "Bring Me To Life" by Evanescence 2. Slam-dunking a basketball 3. "Creep" by Radiohead and "Creep" by TLC 4. Gymnasts 5. *Take A Good Look* 6. Truman Capote 7. The steel industry 8. Soccer 9. Basildon 10. Janitor

Quiz 15: 1. Amy Adams 2. The Finger Lakes 3. Ricky Gervais 4. Ray Romano 5. Josh Groban 6. Kevin McHale 7. Seth Meyers and Bill Hader 8. Ken Jeong 9. Broccoli Rob 10. Joan Cusack and Ed Begley Jr

Quiz 16: 1. Monkey 2. Antihistamines 3. Pete 4. Twine 5. Eggshell white 6. Cash 7. Via text message 8. The Hunted 9. A Nike swoosh 10. Comstock

Quiz 17: 1. An iPod 2. Margarita-Karaoke Christmas 3. "Your Body is a Wonderland" by John Mayer 4. Princess Unicorn 5. A rehabilitation center 6. Start pulling out her hair to make a nest 7. Jesus 8. Inside a snowman 9. A porcupine 10. Pennsylvania Dutch Christmas

Quiz 18: 1. Sandals Jamaica 2. Jamaican Jan Sun Princess 3. Craig 4. Six 5. *Maxim* 6. The Twins 7. Foliage 8. A Porsche 9. She videos them having sex and makes him wear a dress 10. Dwight

Quiz 19: 1. A painting of a clown 2. A teapot 3. Casino Night 4. A rest stop 5. Niagara Falls 6. "Public Displays of Affection" 7. Puerto Rico 8. Brian 9. One week 10. Cecilia (Cece) and Phillip

Quiz 20: 1. February 13th 2. Getting married and having babies immediately 3. He gets a job at corporate in New York City 4. Karen 5. Stanley's daughter 6. Darryl 7. Push-ups 8. Thailand 9. A latte 10. Ohio

Quiz 21: 1. Toby 2. One 3. Counting Crows 4. On a HR retreat 5. AJ 6. A Woody doll from *Toy Story* 7. SlumDunder Mifflinaire 8. His neon bar sign 9. In the office stairwell 10. Three years' salary

Quiz 22: 1. For not saving the oil from a can of tuna 2. Mose 3. Night-time 4. Graves 5. Dwide Schrude 6. Gōjū-ryū 7. A 1987 Pontiac Trans Am 8. 103 9. Seventy 10. A circumcision

Quiz 23: 1. The freezer 2. Accounting 3. Robert Lipton 4. A child's size ten 5. Jane Doe 6. *The Da Vinci Code* 7. A kiss on the forehead 8. Five individual sessions of intercourse 9. 82 pounds 10. Because it is a Halwa Chebakia cookie, traditionally served during Ramadan

Quiz 24: 1. An 80s Lincoln Town Car 2. CreedThoughts 3. Asthma 4. Peach Cobbler 5. They have great heroin 6. Printer ink 7. William Charles Schneider 8. Mung beans 9. Sexuality and pus 10. Four

Quiz 25: 1. Sasha 2. A mystery novel 3. The gym 4. Pam's knee 5. 4:58 pm on a Friday 6. Costa Rica 7. A zip line accident 8. The Scranton Strangler 9. Nellie Bertram 10. He gets strangled

Quiz 26: 1. Here Comes Treble 2. He puts his calculator in Jell-O 3. Nard Dog 4. Nellie Bertram 5. Toby's 6. Cornell University 7. *America's Next A Cappella Sensation* 8. An old family engagement ring 9. *Sweeney Todd* 10. Soap

Quiz 27: 1. Chili 2. Three 3. Jokers and Tokers 4. Michael Moore 5. Fitting the most M&M's in his

mouth 6. Season 4 7. Holly 8. Lynn 9. A bar 10. 69

Quiz 28: 1. Liz Claiborne 2. "That One Night" 3. Doris Day 4. Serenity by Jan 5. Smoking and online shopping 6. Astrid 7. Jasmine Windsong 8. Scottsdale 9. The Scranton White Pages 10. Ice skating

Quiz 29: 1. One dollar 2. Lake Wallenpaupack 3. The sails 4. Salesmen and profit centers 5. She's cold 6. Captain Jack 7. Three years 8. June 10th 9. Look at the moon 10. He ties him to the boat railing

Quiz 30: 1. He burns it on a George Foreman Grill 2. Toilet paper 3. Pam 4. Butter 5. Chuck E. Cheese 6. Michael Scott 7. Carbondale 8. Four extra-strength aspirin 9. His father 10. He puts his foot into the CAT scan machine

Quiz 31: 1. A mini fridge from Vance Refrigeration 2. Her mother 3. He coughs 4. His grandfather, who was buried in it 5. Telekinesis 6. Boy Scouts of America 7. Hooters 8. Abraham Lincoln's 9. Seven and Seven with eight maraschino cherries, sugar on the rim, blended if you can 10. Scrantonicity

Quiz 32: 1. Altoids 2. A toaster 3. The Queen of England 4. He wet his pants 5. Uncle Al 6. Pam's dress and her flowers 7. "the fusing of two metals with a hot torch" 8. Easy Rider 9. "Fields of Gold" 10. He finds Uncle Al

Quiz 33: 1. "Don't be an idiot" 2. A bat 3. He rips pages out of a textbook 4. Tourism, food service, railroads and sales 5. His daughter's play is that night 6. Garlic bread 7. The office building 8. Moves his desk to the annex 9. Motel art 10. A Chunky bar

Quiz 34: 1. His barn 2. "Can we speak privately about our relationship?" 3. A Blackberry 4. That she is pregnant 5. A gift basket with a card attached 6. Into a lake 7. Vince Vaughan 8. "plus a little extra ... also I love you" 9. The chocolate turtles 10. "match ... point ... Scott ... game over ... end of game"

Quiz 35: 1. Toby 2. "by a stranger on purpose" 3. He cuts material off his pants 4. Duct tape 5. Creed, Meredith and Oscar 6. Devil's food cake 7. Three hours 8. A pants tent shelter 9. *Battlestar Galactica* 10. Mushrooms

Quiz 36: 1. Her recent breast enhancement surgery 2. Hiya Buddy 3. "My friend Pat took a turn" 4. Jim and Darryl 5. Four million dollars 6. "she could eat the internet" 7. "Nothing short of predominant" 8. Ryan 9. Michael's private diary 10. "He's a nice guy"

Quiz 37: 1. On a bench at the foot of the bed 2. He says he has soft teeth 3. She used to be his babysitter 4. $200 5. Turkey legs and beet salad 6. Osso buco 7. Babe 8. He says that his apartment is flooded 9. He thought he heard an ice cream truck 10. John Wilkes Booth, Lee Harvey Oswald, Osama Bin Laden, John Wayne Gacy and Jeffrey Lionel Dahmer

Quiz 38: 1. She gets time and a half pay 2. If the baby is Jim's 3. Nashua 4. Jim and Dwight 5. They forgot her birthday 6. By singing it to the theme of "Old MacDonald" 7. A hot dog and a burger costume 8. Angela licking her cat 9. "Good morning Viet Nashua" 10. An hour of TV or an hour of napping

Quiz 39: 1. Michael's condo 2. "Just Dance" by Lady Gaga 3. A toilet flushing 4. A pancake luncheon 5. A brothel 6. Paris, London, Beijing and the USA 7. A laptop 8. Rectangular, to represent paper 9. A "rundown" 10. "Take Me Home, Country Roads" by John Denver

Quiz 40: 1. Third grade 2. The Michael Scott Foundation 3. The Michael Gary Scott Reading Room 4. Jim 5. Thirty 6. Laptop batteries 7. Her pregnancy 8. "It could only be you" 9. Four cheques for $1000 each 10. That ninety percent of Scott's Tots will graduate

Quiz 41: 1. Goldenface 2. Stanley, loosely imitating Morgan Freeman's character in *The Shawshank Redemption* 3. Catherine Zeta-Scarn 4. Darryl 5. Cherokee Jack 6. The Funky Cat 7. Dig her up and hump her real good 8. Inside the hockey puck 9. Exploding Toby's character's head 10. "Go puck yourself"

Quiz 42: 1. A candle 2. Professor Copperfield's Miracle Legumes 3. Gasoline 4. Phyllis 5. The Dallas Board Game 6. Bras 7. Creed's harmonica 8. The sprinklers go off 9. Yoda's 10. Colorado

Quiz 43: 1. Deangelo Vickers 2. Wind-up chattering teeth 3. The office shredder 4. Ryan 5. "Catch you on the flippity flop" 6. To let him use the warehouse baler 7. Play paintball 8. *The King's Speech* 9. Under her windshield wiper 10. If the show ever airs

Quiz 44: 1. Meatballs 2. Kevin 3. Susan 4. "And Gabe-y makes three" 5. Two bears 6. She asks him if Darryl can swim 7. A leg of mutton 8. *Caligula, Last Tango in Paris* and *Emmanuelle II* 9. The Bernard family seal 10. Robert jumps into the pool naked

Quiz 45: 1. Austin, Texas 2. An onion loaf 3. Phyllis 4. Meredith's son 5. The trunk of a car 6. Drake 7. Michael 8. "and then they married each other" 9. In the office supply closet 10. *The History of Us*

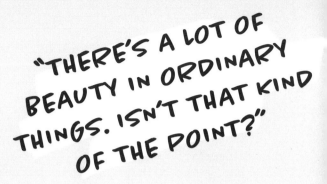

"THERE'S A LOT OF BEAUTY IN ORDINARY THINGS. ISN'T THAT KIND OF THE POINT?"

Smith
Street
Books

Published in 2020 by Smith Street Books
Naarm | Melbourne | Australia
smithstreetbooks.com

ISBN: 978-1-92581-172-8

All rights reserved. No part of this book may be reproduced or transmitted by any person or entity, in any form or means, electronic or mechanical, including photocopying, recording, scanning or by any storage and retrieval system, without the prior written permission of the publishers and copyright holders.

Copyright text & design © Smith Street Books

Publisher: Paul McNally
Text: Amy Lewis
Editor: Aisling Coughlan
Designer: Vanessa Masci
Layout: Megan Ellis

Printed & bound in China by C&C Offset Printing Co., Ltd.

Book 139
10 9 8 7 6 5 4 3